THE CAROLS OF
CHRISTMAS

The Carols Of Christmas

A Celebration of the Christ Child

Erwin W. Lutzer

Moody Church Media
Chicago

Unless othewise indicated, all Scripture quotations are taken from *The Holy Bible,* English Standard Version. ESV® Text Edition: 2016. Copyright © 2001 by Crossway Bibles, a publishing ministry of Good News Publishers.

Cover by Bryan Butler

THE CAROLS OF CHRISTMAS
Copyright © 2019 by Erwin W. Lutzer
Published by Moody Church Media
Chicago, Illinois 60614
www.moodymedia.org

ISBN: 978-1-6956-3565-4

CONTENTS

Dear Friends,

This book is dedicated to all who sing Christmas carols with gratitude and passion—celebrating the Savior who came to redeem us. I have celebrated Christmas for many years, but the wonder and joy of the season returns each Christmas as I sing these hymns. Although I am by no means a musician, I am so blessed by those whom God inspired to write such music and lyrics—carols which continue to bless us to this day, and should the Lord tarry, for generations to come.

Each of the Christmas carols contained in this booklet was written within a context, by a writer who personally experienced the wonder of the Incarnation as given to us in Scripture.

So enjoy this book and sing these familiar carols with new appreciation. I know I will, and I pray you will do the same.

Pastor Lutzer

HYMN ONE:

HARK! THE HERALD ANGELS SING

Charles Wesley

HARK! THE HERALD ANGELS SING

Hark! the herald angels sing,
"Glory to the newborn King;
Peace on earth, and mercy mild,
God and sinners reconciled!"
Joyful, all ye nations, rise,
Join the triumph of the skies;
With the angelic host proclaim,
"Christ is born in Bethlehem!"

Hark! the herald angels sing,
"Glory to the newborn King."

Christ, by highest heaven adored;
Christ, the everlasting Lord!
Late in time behold Him come,
Offspring of the Virgin's womb:
Veiled in flesh the Godhead see;
Hail the incarnate Deity,
Pleased as man with men to dwell,
Jesus, our Emmanuel.

Hark! the herald angels sing,
"Glory to the newborn King."

Hail, the heaven-born Prince of Peace!
Hail, the Sun of Righteousness!
Light and life to all He brings,
Risen with healing in His wings.
Mild He lays His glory by,
Born that men no more may die,
Born to raise the sons of earth,
Born to give them second birth.

Hark! the herald angels sing,
"Glory to the newborn King."

CHAPTER 1

HARK! THE HERALD ANGELS SING

"Hark! The Herald Angels Sing!"

This hymn was written by Charles Wesley, the brother of the famous evangelist John Wesley. The Wesleys were mightily used of God in the English revivals during the 1700s. But they were banned from the Anglican Church because they disagreed with some of the doctrines of the church, and because their methods were different from those of other preachers.

Charles is also the author of other hymns such as "Love Divine, All Loves Excelling," and a couple other of my favorites, "And Can It Be That I Should Gain An Interest In My Savior's Blood?" and "Jesus, Lover Of My Soul."

Yet, "Hark! The Herald Angels Sing" was the only song written by Charles Wesley that made it into the Church of England's *Book of Common Prayer*. There is a story, perhaps true, that a printer needed one more hymn to fit into the hymnal and thus this song was added. Attempts were made to remove the hymn, but because of its popularity, it was allowed to remain.

Though "Hark! The Herald Angels Sing" first appeared as ten stanzas with four lines each, today it has four stanzas with ten lines each. Wesley often wrote his hymns quickly, without polishing them. There have been many alterations throughout the years, though we can be sure that the gist of the original has been retained.

This Christmas carol would probably have remained in relative obscurity were it not for the fact that in 1840, Germany's boy wonder, Felix Mendelssohn, wrote an opera which later included the song. This popularized it and gave it a permanent position in the hearts of millions. Today it stands as one of our best loved Christmas carols.

To "hark" means to listen. The angels invite us to join them in praise to Christ. And the message they brought changed the world forever. "And suddenly there was with the angel a multitude of the heavenly host praising God and saying, 'Glory to God in the highest, and on earth peace among those with whom he is pleased!'" (Luke 2:13–14).

Luke wants us to understand that the angel appeared when it was dark; the shepherds were watching their flocks "by night." The angels arrested the attention of these men with news that would change the world forever. We do well to "hark," that is, to listen with care at the message they brought that night.

We can identify with the fear of the shepherds. When the first angel appeared, we read, "the glory of the Lord shone around them, and they were filled with great fear" (Luke 2:9). We would have also been frightened by this heavenly apparition. We would have been frightened to see a light brighter than the sun—the very light of a holy God. This mighty blaze lit up the heavens and turned midnight into midday. This was the shekinah glory, the heavenly light, the manifestation of God. The last time it appeared in Israel was when the temple was destroyed and the glory disappeared over the Mount of Olives. And now it returns to the outskirts of Bethlehem!

That cloud of glory exposes the sin of humanity. It is also the cloud that led God's people in the desert. This return of glory in Bethlehem was a sign that the curse of the last 400 years was lifted and the presence of God had returned to encourage and bless. Now the angels sing of this glory. *Glory to God in the highest!*

The angels had been present at creation. They had seen Jehovah fashion the planets; they had seen many a star tossed into the endless reaches of space. But this time when they saw God step from His throne and become a baby, they lifted their voices higher in praise because the Redeemer had been born.

God is glorified in every drop of water; He is magnified in every flower. He is glorified in every bird that sings; "But sing O universe till thou has exhausted thyself, thou canst not afford a song as sweet as the incarnation," said Charles Haddon Spurgeon. We echo his sentiments.

Indeed, the song of creation is glorious, but the song of redemption exceeds far beyond that glory. What justice is here: God has become man that he might be just and the "justifier of the one who has faith in Jesus" (Romans 3:26). What power is here, as God lays aside His glory and becomes a man; behold, what faithfulness, what love. What wisdom is found in that one person who is both the Son of Man and the Son of God.

Again I quote Spurgeon, "All the attributes of God were in that little child most marvelously displayed and veiled. Conceive the whole sun to be focused to a single point and yet so softly revealed as to be durable by the most tender eye, even thus the glorious God is brought down for man to see him born of a woman." Well might the angels call us to attention.

Joy was offered to the shepherds to replace their fear. "Do not be afraid" the angel assures them. "Behold, I bring you good news of great joy" (Luke 2:10). We are invited to join the shepherds and shake off our fears. Fear came into this world because of sin. Before they sinned, Adam and Eve had no fears; after they sinned they were afraid and "hid themselves from the presence of the Lord God among the trees of the garden" (Genesis 3:8).

We are, by nature, enemies of God and have every reason to fear Him. But we also fear one another; we fear the future, we fear violence, and we fear old age. We fear loneliness and sickness. Meet any person and he will have secret fears. Some of these fears might be proper. Fear of God's judgment should make us flee to Christ who shelters us from His wrath.

But fear of death, poverty, violence, and sickness is quite another matter. If we believe that Christ came to reconcile us to God, we know that the most important questions in our lives have been answered. Christ has enabled us to prepare for eternity, thus we are quite ready to deal with the struggles in what we call time. If we need no longer fear death, we need fear nothing else.

Why can we cease fearing? "Behold, I bring you good news of great joy that will be for all the people. For unto you is born this day in the city of David a Savior, who is Christ the Lord" (Luke 2:10–11). Christ has come to take God's enemies and win them over as friends. God had no obligation to do so. The birth of Christ causes us to rejoice because God has come to be reconciled to us. We are not utterly cursed, for God has become one of us.

When the angel said "a Savior has been born for you," he was announcing that God had, as it were, married into the race; the Son of God had become the Son of man. God has not united Himself to any other creature. God has united Himself with us so that He has become our brother. What great thoughts and love He has toward humanity. As Spurgeon said, "If a king's son marries a rebel, then for that rebel race there are profound prospects of reconciliation. The Incarnation bodes well for our race. The baby in Bethlehem means that God intends blessing for us."

The nature of man and the nature of God need not be permanent enemies if God has taken human nature to Himself. The infinite gulf between us and God has been bridged. We have a God who hears us; a God who seeks our reconciliation.

"For unto us is born a Savior..." Those who will rejoice the most are those who know that they are sinners. If an angel had come to save us, we might have reason to rejoice. But the even better news is that God, the infinite, the Almighty has come to be our Savior. In the Old Testament, God had come to Mount Sinai to reveal His Law; He came to disobedient Israelites as an avenger. Only now did He come as a Savior. God's omnipotence has condescended to our feebleness. Infinite majesty has stooped to our infirmity.

"And on earth peace among those with whom he is pleased!" (Luke 2:14). Wars have filled the world. There are wars within as well as wars without. There has been no peace on Earth since Adam fell. But now in Bethlehem Christ came in the white bands of peace.

True, there is no peace in the world today; but peace

there shall be. The Prince of Peace will return to set the record straight. But until then, there can be peace in our hearts. "Peace I leave with you; my peace I give to you" (John 14:27a) Christ assures us.

To quote Spurgeon once more, "That manger was the place where the treaty was signed, whereby war should be stopped between man's conscience and himself; between man's conscience and his God." No greater act of kindness could be offered from God to us than that He should offer His Son to us.

What would it have been like if Christ had not come? Moral decay without remedy; suffering without comfort; war without peace; guilt without forgiveness; death without hope. Take this Christ-child away and peace becomes impossible. Take Him away and joy becomes a mirage.

Hark! The herald angels sing!

I stand amazed at the delight of the angels. They rejoice though they derive no direct benefit from Christ's coming. These are the righteous angels, those who stand before God and sing His praises. Their eternal destiny was not at stake. Whether Christ had come to Earth or not, their relationship with God was secure and fulfilling. Yet how they delight in the coming of God's Son!

The angels rejoice for us. They are wholly free from all envy. They rejoice when one sinner repents and takes advantage of Christ's coming. They are friends of Christ and therefore rejoice when He rejoices. And they rejoice when we rejoice. After the first angel came to the shepherds, I think God could scarcely restrain the others from joining him. "And suddenly there was with the angel a multitude of the heavenly host…" (Luke 2:13).

But if the birth of Jesus was so captivating to our created cousins, what should it be for us? If heaven opened its gates to let a million of God's hosts come to Bethlehem for worship, what should it do for us who are redeemed by the Incarnation?

You are so lonely in the world, but Christ is your brother. You who have sinned so greatly you think you cannot live with yourself, come to Christ. With the disciples, hurry to Bethlehem. For the baby grew up and became our Savior.

In 1955, Don Richardson dedicated himself to becoming a missionary to the head-hunting tribes of New Guinea. He was sent to a tribe that combined cannibalism, head-hunting, and treachery. He agonized over the question of how they could ever come to understand that a loving Savior died for them. In their eyes, Judas, not Jesus, was the hero of the salvation story.

Then Don discovered the key that would unlock the door to their understanding. When he and his wife were about to relocate because their friendship with some of the Sawi tribe was causing open warfare among three other tribes, the leaders persuaded the couple to stay, saying that they would make peace among themselves.

Visualize the peace ceremony: a young child from each of the warring tribes was exchanged. As long as any of those children lived, peace would continue. The decision as to whose child would be exchanged was wrenching indeed. Mothers clutched their children, hoping that theirs would not be selected. Finally, a young father grabbed his only child and rushed toward the enemy camp and gave his son to one of his enemies. He, in turn, received a child from the hands of an enemy. It was a peace based on trust; a tribe that exalted treachery believed that only when a man gave his son could he be trusted.

Just so, God gave us His Son. We, however, gave Him no child in return. In fact, we killed His Son. Yet even the death of His beloved Son did not cause Him to turn His back on us, but actually this crime became a part of the redemptive story. Salvation is all one-sided; we do the sinning, He does the saving. And although we abused His Son, He reminds us that even this was a part of the redemptive plan.

That night on the outskirts of Bethlehem, the shepherds were told that they would not discover Him in the halls of princes, nor in the golden cradle of a king's palace. The King arrived with a peasant for a mother and a carpenter for His foster-father. "For unto you is born this day in the city of David a Savior, who is Christ the Lord" (Luke 2:11).

Though there were many other people in the country that night, only a few shepherds were invited to see the Christ. Today, our responsibility is to spread the word everywhere, *Christ has come; He invites us, not to a stable, but to a cross and an empty tomb!* How slow we are to worship! How reluctant our world is to join the shepherds adoring the Christ.

When the angels sang, "Glory to God in the highest, and on earth peace among those with whom he is pleased!" (Luke 2:14) the good news was limited to those who would accept the gift of Christ. Not all men benefit from Christ's coming, but only those who experience the favor of God— only those who know Christ as Savior come under the shelter of His grace and protection.

> *Hail, the heaven-born Prince of Peace!*
> *Hail, the Sun of Righteousness!*
> *Light and life to all He brings,*
> *Risen with healing in His wings.*
> *Mild He lays His glory by,*
> *Born that men no more may die,*
> *Born to raise the sons of earth,*
> *Born to give them second birth.*
>
> *Hark! the herald angels sing,*
> *"Glory to the newborn King."*

HYMN TWO:
SILENT NIGHT!
HOLY NIGHT!

Joseph Mohr

SILENT NIGHT! HOLY NIGHT!

Silent night, holy night,
All is calm, all is bright
Round yon virgin mother and Child.
Holy Infant so tender and mild,
Sleep in heavenly peace,
Sleep in heavenly peace.

Silent night, holy night,
Shepherds quake at the sight.
Glories stream from heaven afar;
Heavenly hosts sing alleluia.
Christ the Savior is born!
Christ the Savior is born!

Silent night, holy night,
Son of God, love's pure light
Radiant beams from Thy holy face,
With the dawn of redeeming grace,
Jesus, Lord, at Thy birth,
Jesus, Lord, at Thy birth.

CHAPTER 2

SILENT NIGHT! HOLY NIGHT!

On Christmas Eve, 1818, in the village of Oberndorf near Salzburg, Joseph Mohr, a 22-year-old clergyman faced the task of telling the congregation in Saint Nicholas Church that the organ was broken; and though it could not be repaired by Christmas, he was optimistic that there would, nevertheless, be music on Christmas Day. The rumor was that the mice had eaten through the bellows, and a repairman was not able to fix them immediately.

Franz Gruber, the organist, was despondent over the broken organ, but was encouraged by Joseph Mohr's hope that there would be music in the church on Christmas Day. Both Mohr and Gruber loved music and lightheartedness so much so that Mohr, who was actually an assistant priest at the church, was believed by some to not take his duties as seriously as he should.

On Christmas Eve, Mohr made a pastoral visit; he called on a young woodcutter who celebrated the birth of a newborn baby. That evening on his way home, he began to contemplate the birth of Christ. He walked to the top of a hill, looked at the town against the background of a star-lit evening. Words came to him that he rushed home to record:

> *"Stille Nacht*
> *Heilige Nacht*
> *Alles schalft*
> *Einsam wacht"*

The next morning, he hurried over to Gruber's home and gave the words to him as a Christmas gift. "God be praised!" said Gruber. "We have often expressed sorrow that the perfect Christmas hymn had not been written and now we have it!"

"Write the music for it!" Mohr told him. Gruber thought that this was impossible with the organ broken, but he was reminded he could use his guitar.

That evening at their Christmas service, they sang the song as a duet. It was an instant success, and when the organ repairman, Karl Mauracher, came in the spring of that year (1819), he asked Gruber to play a song. Of course he chose "Silent Night." The repairman was captivated by it and helped spread the song throughout the churches and villages.

Later it was used by the Strasser family, a children's

quartet who sang at the Leipzig fair. Twenty-two years after it had been written, it was performed by a choir for King Frederick William IV of Prussia who ordered it be given first place in all future Christmas concerts within the bounds of his domain.

As for Joseph Mohr, an illegitimate child, he died of tuberculosis at the age of 46 never knowing that he had given the world its favorite Christmas carol. It was translated into English in 1863 and was used in an English hymnal in 1871. Today, it is translated and sung in 120 different languages.

Why are we so captivated by that particular "Silent Night, Holy Night?" We are intrigued by the fact that a Roman Emperor 1,500 miles away started the train of events that finally led to the birth of Christ in Bethlehem. Augustus decreed that there be a census within his vast empire. All subjects had to return to their ancestral home towns to be registered. So it was that an obscure Galilean couple had to obey a distant Caesar. He now requested this enrollment to assess the population of the Empire and to levy new taxes.

Dr. Paul Maier invites us to speculate how Augustus would have reacted to these three names from Bethlehem had he seen them in the Roman register:

Joseph, son of Jacob, carpenter;

Mary, his wife;

Yeshua, or Jesus, first-born son.

The names would have been meaningless. The great emperor died in AD 14 when Jesus would have been a teenager, an apprentice carpenter in Nazareth. Caesar would have been astounded to know that the ages would assign his own death as "in the year of our Lord" AD 14, rather than using the Roman calendar.

In Nazareth, Joseph and Mary's wedding plans were interrupted. Gabriel appeared to Mary and promised she would give birth to a King who would sit on the throne of David. Mary submitted in simple trust, "let it be to me according to your word" (Luke 1:38).

This prospect was both joyful and staggering. She knew that all generations would call her blessed, but her pregnancy was shocking news to Joseph, for he knew that he was not the father of the child. He found her story hard to believe, so he agonized: should he have a quick marriage? Or should he publicly divorce her as an adulteress, in which case she could have been stoned to death? He chose a third alternative, namely to put her away privately. But an angel came to him in a dream and told him that he should take her as his wife, "for that which is conceived in her is from the Holy Spirit" (Matthew 1:20).

Probably no more than a week or two later, the wedding was celebrated in Nazareth. Mary and Joseph would have marched in procession, accompanied by music to the place of the ceremony. They would have had attendants and a banquet.

For the next five months, Mary lived in Joseph's house, her pregnancy now obvious. However much they dreaded a four or five day trip to Bethlehem, the decree solved two problems: the baby would be born in Bethlehem where no one knew them, shielding them from the sneers and whispers of their friends. And second, it would fulfill Micah's prophecy.

The picture of Joseph guiding the donkey for the five or six day journey is engraved in our imaginations. How he hoped and prayed that the birth pangs would not come until they arrived where the Scriptures said they should be! Only a mother can understand the discomforts that Mary would have felt on that journey.

Why do we retell the Christmas story every year and never grow tired of it? Why do we love the song, "Silent Night, Holy Night"?

First, it's because we are impressed with how silently God entered our world. That He would choose an ordinary peasant girl to be taken to an ordinary town, where her Child would be born in an ordinary stable, and laid in an ordinary manger, mystifies us.

Could you imagine if, when she was about to give birth to Prince William, Princess Diana discovered that all the hospitals and motels in London were filled? I doubt she would have been shown to a cave where cattle were housed. Even the poor deserve better; but how much more royalty!

God slipped in with no one noticing. He came without fanfare; the world slept, the Redeemer was born, and the next day, nothing changed! God really did enter our world. The smell of the cave, the child in the manger is proof of that. That is why we sing, "Silent Night, Holy Night."

Second, we are impressed with how personally God entered our world. He didn't send a representative to do the dirty work. He didn't send an angel to come to be humiliated and die. He did it Himself.

Walter Wangerin tells the story of how he often looked into the face of his adopted biracial daughter and wondered what the mother and father looked like. He wondered if he would recognize them if he saw them on the street (CT, December 1995). No doubt Joseph spent hours looking into the face of the little boy at his table and wondered what His Father was like. He was looking into the face of God.

Finally, we are impressed with how graciously God entered the world. He didn't have to do it. There was no logical necessity; there was no moral necessity. But He did it. He bridged the gap between us and Himself. He brought forgiveness and showed us how to forgive each other.

During World War II, three American soldiers wandered into German territory without knowing it.

They were spotted by some Germans and a brief shoot out ensued. One of the Americans had a bullet lodged in his body. The other two GIs dragged him to a small cottage where they asked a woman and her daughter to take care of them for the night. They reluctantly agreed.

Hours later, there was a knock on the door and German soldiers arrived at the same house. The woman explained that she already had guests, though she added that they were guests of which the Germans might not approve.

When the Germans insisted that they come in with their weapons, the woman said, "No. This is Christmas Eve...cannot we at least have peace at Christmas?" She invited them in on one condition: that the Germans, as well as the Americans, leave their weapons outside her door. Reluctantly, all agreed.

The woman prepared a meal for both the German and American soldiers. The wounded American lay groaning, obviously in pain. Though the communication between the English-speaking soldiers and the Germans was difficult, one of the German soldiers agreed to perform basic emergency surgery on the American. He successfully removed the bullet.

And then the soldiers sang together, in English and German:

Silent night, holy night,
All is calm, all is bright

Round yon virgin mother and Child.
Holy Infant so tender and mild,
Sleep in heavenly peace,
Sleep in heavenly peace.

The next morning, the Germans gave the Americans a map so that they might be able to find their way back to the rest of their army; then they went on their way. And, of course, after Christmas, the shooting began again. But for one brief moment, the message of Christmas and the words of a song brought enemies together. For one brief moment, the antagonists forgot their weapons and remembered that there was a message that could unite them.

That's what God says to us. God says because My Son has come, you can leave your weapons at the door. You can come in and we can have fellowship together. Christ was born to die; born to reconcile us to God. And He does that for all who believe in Him. We can be thankful for that special night in Bethlehem.

Silent night, holy night,
Shepherds quake at the sight.
Glories stream from heaven afar;
Heavenly hosts sing alleluia.
Christ the Savior is born!
Christ the Savior is born!

ERWIN W. LUTZER

HYMN THREE:

WHO IS HE
IN YONDER STALL?

Benjamin Russell Hanby

WHO IS HE IN YONDER STALL?

Who is He in yonder stall,
At whose feet the shepherds fall?
Who is He in deep distress,
Fasting in the wilderness?

'Tis the Lord! O wondrous story!
'Tis the Lord! the King of glory!
At His feet we humbly fall,
Crown Him! crown Him, Lord of all!

Who is He the people bless
For His words of gentleness?
Who is He to whom they bring
All the sick and sorrowing?

'Tis the Lord! O wondrous story!
'Tis the Lord! the King of glory!
At His feet we humbly fall,
Crown Him! crown Him, Lord of all!

Who is He that stands and weeps
At the grave where Lazarus sleeps?
Who is He the gath'ring throng
Greet with loud triumphant song?

'Tis the Lord! O wondrous story!
'Tis the Lord! the King of glory!
At His feet we humbly fall,
Crown Him! crown Him, Lord of all!

Lo! at midnight, who is He
Prays in dark Gethsemane?
Who is He on yonder tree
Dies in grief and agony?

'Tis the Lord! O wondrous story!
'Tis the Lord! the King of glory!
At His feet we humbly fall,
Crown Him! crown Him, Lord of all!

Who is He that from the grave
Comes to heal and help and save?
Who is He that from His throne
Rules through all the world alone?

'Tis the Lord! O wondrous story!
'Tis the Lord! the King of glory!
At His feet we humbly fall,
Crown Him! crown Him, Lord of all!

CHAPTER 3

WHO IS HE IN YONDER STALL?

"Who Is He In Yonder Stall?"

You have probably sung this Christmas carol many times. It just happens to be one of my favorites. This hymn was written by Benjamin Russell Hanby (1833–1867) who published music in Chicago.

Although the song is a Christmas carol, it covers all the important events in Christ's life and therefore could be sung at any time of the year. The song speaks of Christ's ministry, death, and resurrection. Hanby raises the question as to who Christ is and then answers it.

'Tis the Lord! O wondrous story!
'Tis the Lord! the King of glory!
At His feet we humbly fall,
Crown Him! crown Him, Lord of all!

So, who is He in yonder stall? Some would answer, "A harmless baby." That is why so many people love Him;

everyone loves a baby. A baby is not a threat to our lives and existence. Babies don't order us to rearrange our priorities; babies don't make us face our sins and tell us how to be right with God. As long as Christ is thought of as just a baby in a manger, He will be loved with benign sentimentality.

Who is He in yonder stall? If the merchants of Christmas were to answer that question honestly, they would say, "He is a marketable commodity." Because He is good for business, the world adores the baby in the manger. Have you ever wondered what Christ thinks of His birthday party? Gifts for everyone except the One who is supposedly being honored!

Never mind that the Christ of the New Testament, were He physically present, would expose the greed of commercialism; never mind that the One whose birthday we celebrate would chide us for using His birthday as an opportunity to enrich ourselves.

Who is He in yonder stall? Millions of others would reply that He is simply a remarkable teacher. He is a good man, they say, who helped the poor and showed that He loved us; a man who went about doing good but was misunderstood.

So who is He in yonder stall? Yes, He was a baby, but not anymore. In fact, the reason we celebrate His birth is because of who He turned out to be.

Let's let Him tell us who He is.

That baby, now a man, gives His final words in the closing verses of the book of Revelation (see 22:13–16). He uses three figures of speech to help us grasp who He really is.

First, there is an alphabetical figure. "I am the Alpha and the Omega, the first and the last" (Revelation 22:13). That word, "alpha," is the first letter of the Greek alphabet; the word, "omega," is the last letter. Christ is saying that He is the A to Z, the beginning and the end. We should not be surprised that this same figure of speech is used by God the Father earlier in the book, "'I am the Alpha and the Omega,' says the Lord God, 'who is and who was and who is to come, the Almighty'" (Revelation 1:8).

In using this figure of speech, Christ is claiming to be God. Someone has paraphrased it, "I am He from whom all being has proceeded and to whom it will return."

He is the Alpha. Let your imagination journey back in time long before the universe was created, long before the angels were spoken into existence. Think of a time when God was alone; Christ was there. He is the Eternal One, the Everlasting Father, the Prince of Peace. As the Beginning, He is the Creator. Colossians 1:16, "For by him all things were created." Today, the Son maintains the unity and existence of creation. He is the one who "upholds the universe by the word of his power" (Hebrews 1:3).

He is also the Omega, proof that He will also exist in the future. He has existed throughout the entire chain of events that we call history. And in the end, He shall rule in victory and power. And throughout all of eternity, He will be seated on the throne, ruling in the heavens.

And we are now as eternal as Christ. We did not exist in eternity past, but we will be there in eternity future. He graciously allows us to enjoy His future; we do not have within ourselves the cause of our existence, but He sustains us and gives us eternal life.

The Encyclopedia Britannica has more than thirty volumes of material, including science, history, and philosophy. Yet all of this knowledge is written with just 26 letters of the alphabet. Christ is the Alpha and Omega, He is the One in whom is contained "all the treasures of wisdom and knowledge" (Colossians 2:3).

Who is He in yonder stall? At Whose feet the shepherds fall? The alphabetical figure of speech answers: Christ the Lord…the First and the Last, the Beginning and the End. No wonder he can continue, "Blessed are those who wash their robes, that they may have the right to the tree of life, and may enter by the gates into the city" (see Revelation 7, 21, and 22). And what about those who do not gain access to the city? They will be forever banished from the glorious cosmic celebration.

Who is He in yonder stall? The Creator of the stall in which He was born. The owner of the inn from which He was turned away—God, to be precise. The One who is the

Creator of the Holy City and the One who determines who can or cannot enter within its gates.

Next, He uses a botanical figure of speech. He is the "root and the descendant of David" (Revelation 22:16). Consider that for a moment. He is the Root of David because He is the One who gave David his life. He is the Father of David. In human terms, we think of the line of David which eventually gave birth to Christ. But here, Christ, as it were, is giving birth to David. He is the Root from which David has sprung.

Yet here is where it gets tricky. Yes, Christ is the offspring of David. In 2 Samuel 7, God gave David a promise that he would have a son who would rule forever. And when the angel came to Mary, the promise was that "He will be great and will be called the Son of the Most High. And the Lord God will give to him the throne of his father David, and he will reign over the house of Jacob forever, and of his kingdom there will be no end" (Luke 1:32–33). Christ is the offspring of David, yet He is also David's Creator, David's God.

Think about this puzzle Christ used to silence His critics. The Pharisees wanted to entrap Him in His own words, but Christ turned the tables. He asked them, "What do you think about the Christ? Whose son is he?" They replied, "The son of David" (Matthew 22:42).

Then Christ went on to ask, "How is it then that David,

in the Spirit, calls him Lord, saying, 'The Lord said to my Lord, Sit at my right hand, until I put your enemies under your feet'?" Now here comes the clincher: "If then David calls him Lord, how is he his son?" (Matthew 22:43–45). The answer, of course, is that He is both David's Lord and David's son. In the flesh, He is the son of David; in the Spirit, He is God.

No wonder the Pharisees who would not submit to Christ refused to debate the point. We simply read, "And no one was able to answer him a word, nor from that day did anyone dare to ask him any more questions" (v. 46).

Here we have the supreme paradox: deity had joined with humanity; the two natures were inseparably united without mixture or loss of their complete separate identity. This is the unfathomable mystery of the Incarnation. Here we are at the heart of the Christmas story.

Who is He in yonder stall? Who is He in deep distress, fasting in the wilderness? The answer of the botanical figure says, "It is Christ the Son of man, and Christ the Son of God."

Third, Christ gives an astronomical figure. He refers to Himself as the "bright morning star" (Revelation 22:16). Astronomy must surely be the most interesting of all the sciences. Stars upon stars, galaxies upon galaxies. You can buy a star for a friend as a Christmas present. The person who thought of selling the stars should get a prize for ingenuity. You can see your gift on a dark night, but you can't take it home with you!

A star is symbolic of kingship. For example, in Numbers 24:17 we read, "I see him, but not now; I behold him, but not near: a star shall come out of Jacob, and a scepter shall rise out of Israel; it shall crush the forehead of Moab and break down all the sons of Sheth." In the New Testament, Christ is referred to as the sun, "because of the tender mercy of our God, whereby the sunrise shall visit us from on high to give light to those who sit in darkness and in the shadow of death, to guide our feet into the way of peace" (Luke 1:78–79).

In the literature of the ancient Middle East, kings were often designated as stars. The kings of the East came to Bethlehem saying that they had seen His star in the east and had come to worship Him. He is indeed the "star of all stars."

While he walked on Earth, Christ's face was often wet with tears as He pled for men and women to repent. He got hungry and thirsty and became weary with His travels. But now, He is the brightest star in the universe. He who appeared so ordinary during His time on Earth now radiates glory we cannot see, for no man could see Him and live. This God-man who spoke so tenderly when on Earth will someday tell men, "Depart from me, all ye workers of iniquity" (Luke 13:27 KJV).

A star is also symbolic of a guide. The stars, since they remain fixed even during storms, were used for navigation and direction as wanderers crossed the broad plains and deserts. The traveler always had a true reading on his position. Christ, the star, is the only One qualified to guide us successfully all the way home. He could say, "I am the way, and the truth, and the life. No one comes to the Father except through me" (John 14:6).

"Who is He in yonder stall? Who is He the gathering throng, greet with loud triumphant song?" Benjamin Hanby was right:

> 'Tis the Lord! O wondrous story!
> 'Tis the Lord! the King of glory!
> At His feet we humbly fall,
> Crown Him! crown Him, Lord of all!

Appropriately, the book of Revelation closes with a final invitation. Just as our bodies need water, so our souls must be satisfied by the One qualified to bring us to God. "The Spirit and the Bride say, 'Come.' And let the one who hears say, 'Come.' And let the one who is thirsty come; let the one who desires take the water of life without price" (Revelation 22:17). The Spirit says "Come!" He is inviting Christ's return. The bride, that is the church, says, "Come!" We are as excited as a bride on her wedding day, anticipating the permanent love of her groom. We are making ourselves ready for the marriage supper of the Lamb; little wonder we, the church say, "Come!" Finally, the individual sitting in church and hearing the book of Revelation read, the "one who hears," he also longs for Christ's return and says, "Come!"

All of these long for the coming of the One who was a baby in "yonder stall." How different our Christmas celebrations would be if we remembered whose birth we celebrate. Yes, we worship a baby, but He is a baby who has become a man. He is a man about to be the Judge, a Judge prepared to rule directly as King.

Little wonder John says, "Even so, come, Lord Jesus."

HYMN FOUR:

O LITTLE TOWN OF BETHLEHEM

Phillips Brooks

ERWIN W. LUTZER

O LITTLE TOWN OF BETHLEHEM

O little town of Bethlehem,
How still we see thee lie!
Above thy deep and dreamless sleep
The silent stars go by.
Yet in thy dark streets shineth
The everlasting Light;
The hopes and fears of all the years
Are met in thee tonight.

For Christ is born of Mary,
And gathered all above,
While mortals sleep, the angels keep
Their watch of wond'ring love.
O morning stars, together
Proclaim the holy birth;
And praises sing to God, the King,
And peace to men on earth.

How silently, how silently
The wondrous Gift is giv'n!
So God imparts to human hearts
The blessings of His heav'n.

No ear may hear His coming,
But in this world of sin,
Where meek souls will receive Him still,
The dear Christ enters in.

O holy Child of Bethlehem,
Descend to us, we pray.
Cast out our sin, and enter in;
Be born in us today.
We hear the Christmas angels
The great glad tidings tell.
O come to us, abide with us,
Our Lord, Emmanuel.

CHAPTER 4

O LITTLE TOWN OF BETHLEHEM

Bethlehem has been given world-wide fame. It has a special place in the heart of every Christian. There are different reasons why some places have prominence. For example, some buildings are famous because of the people who design them; people come to Chicago from all over the world to see the architecture of Frank Lloyd Wright. Some buildings are famous because of who lives in them; we think of Buckingham Palace, the residence of kings and queens. Some places are famous because of who was born there. Such is Bethlehem.

Travel agents would not have been interested in Bethlehem. Athens had its philosophers, Rome had its power, Jerusalem its temple. Bethlehem had nothing noteworthy; it was always overshadowed by its famous neighbor, the glorious city of Jerusalem.

Were it not for the birth of Christ, Bethlehem would never have gained recognition. But today, this little town has a tender spot in all of our hearts. Even those who have never visited Bethlehem think of it with a warm sense of appreciation.

When Phillips Brooks was the rector of the Holy Trinity Episcopal Church in Philadelphia, he was asked to write a song for their Christmas celebration in 1868. He had been brought up in a pious New England home where the children had to memorize hymns for family devotions. He had come to know about 200 by memory.

Now, with the challenge of writing a song before him, he recalled an experience he had in Palestine. On Christmas Eve he stood on a hillside overlooking Bethlehem, imagining the story of Mary and Joseph and the baby. He visualized the couple being turned away because others, more important, had made "advance reservations." He almost thought he could hear the angels singing on the outskirts of the town. That night, he attended a Christmas Eve service in the Church of the Nativity.

Back in Philadelphia, Brooks prayed, "O holy Child of Bethlehem! Descend to us we pray; cast out our sin and enter in; be born in us today." He realized that Christ was still being rejected though He came to help us, not to hurt us.

Brooks wrote the words of the song and gave them to his organist, Lewis H. Redner, who hoped to write the music by Christmas Eve. But as the days passed, he simply could not create the right tune. Then one night he awoke, and the music came to him quickly. He always referred to this inspiration as a "gift from heaven."

Most people know very little about Phillips Brooks who died in 1893, but his hymn lives on.

O little town of Bethlehem.

Why Bethlehem?

First, the word "Bethlehem" means "house of bread." The book of Ruth opens, "There was a famine in the house of bread." Bread is one of the most perfect foods; it represents the staples of life. Spiritual bread is to the soul what physical bread is to the body. Christ said, "Do not work for the food that perishes, but for the food that endures to eternal life" (John 6:27). And again, "'Truly, truly, I say to you, it was not Moses who gave you the bread from heaven, but my Father gives you the true bread from heaven. For the bread of God is he who comes down from heaven and gives life to the world.' They said to him, 'Sir, give us this bread always'" (v. 32–34).

Physical bread is important only now; the spiritual bread is necessary for eternity. "I am the bread of life; whoever comes to me shall not hunger, and whoever believes in me shall never thirst" (v. 35). Christ's bread is more important, just as eternity is more important than time. Thankfully, He came to the manger that we might eat our fill.

Bethlehem isn't called the "house of water" but it could

have been. Remember how David longed for the water from the pools of Bethlehem. Three men heard his whisper and said to themselves, "If David wants water, we'll risk our lives to get it." David took the water and poured it on the ground; he said in effect, "This isn't water, it is blood." So he gave it as an offering to the Lord (the story is recorded in 2 Samuel 23:15–17).

Perhaps this helps us explain why God chose Bethlehem. The fields of grain produced the bread, and the wells of water refreshed the citizens of the community. Christ is the grain in the fields and the well of water that slakes our thirst.

Bethlehem is also a royal city. It is the "city of David," the man who was Israel's second but most famous king. He was born in or near Bethlehem, in a modest abode. Here he grew up, learned to herd sheep and play on his harp. In later years, David was promised a son who would rule on his throne forever. "When your days are fulfilled and you lie down with your fathers, I will raise up your offspring after you, who shall come from your body, and I will establish his kingdom" (2 Samuel 7:12). It only makes sense that David's special son would be born in the same town where he himself was born and lived.

The angel predicted to Mary that Christ would be a greater king than David. Indeed He would "reign over the house of Jacob forever, and of his kingdom there will be no end" (Luke 1:33). The primary purpose of the book of Ruth is to trace the genealogy of the line of David so that the fulfillment of God's promise would be seen.

Perhaps another reason why Bethlehem was chosen is because it is a town of suffering. The first time it is mentioned is when Rachel died there while giving birth to Benjamin (Genesis 35:11 ff). In Hebrew, his name was given as Ben-oni, "son of sorrow," but his father called him Benjamin, "the son of my right hand."

Bethlehem has seen its share of conflict, heartache, and death. Read the Old Testament and you will discover that wars have often been fought here. King Herod killed all the male children two years of age and younger in the area around Bethlehem, hoping to kill the Christ child. Even today Bethlehem is a powder keg that could erupt in a brutal war. Fitting, isn't it, that one should be born here who is "a man of sorrows and acquainted with grief" (see Isaiah 53).

Bethlehem was also the overlooked city. It was "too little to be among the clans of Judah" (Micah 5:2). That means that it was too insignificant to appear on Joshua's list of conquered cities. Jericho we know, Jerusalem we know, but where is Bethlehem? Geographically it is about five miles south of Jerusalem, the bigger city that got all of the attention (and still does).

If you had lived in Bethlehem, you would have learned

to adjust to low expectations. You would likely have settled in and become content, knowing that you will never be number one. Probably no one bragged about being from Bethlehem. If you wanted to make a name for yourself, you would have to go elsewhere.

Bethlehem was the unlikely city. If God had wanted to stage a grand entrance into the world, He could have chosen Rome, or Athens, or Jerusalem. He chose a city known for its obscurity and elevated it to a position of prominence.

God's choices are unpredictable. No one would have predicted that the Redeemer's birth would be in Bethlehem. The Spirit of God revealed it to the prophet Micah, but apart from such revelation, Bethlehem would not have been on the short list.

Someone observed that the "most likely to succeed" are often found to be the "least likely to succeed" twenty years later. Someone told me, "I have given up trying to predict those whom God will greatly use." If you are overlooked and obscure, you just might be the kind of person God will choose for some mighty great things.

The gap from Earth to heaven already approached infinity, but God deliberately made the gap even wider by choosing Bethlehem over other more viable options.

Christ came to Bethlehem…that was an act of grace. Christ was born "King of the Jews." I don't know if anyone else ever was born a king; most had to wait to be crowned.

But Christ came as the king. He came to Bethlehem that He might come to us. If we ask, "Why Bethlehem?" we should really ask, "Why us?" Let us sing with Phillips Brooks:

> *O holy Child of Bethlehem,*
> *Descend to us, we pray.*
> *Cast out our sin, and enter in;*
> *Be born in us today.*
> *We hear the Christmas angels*
> *The great glad tidings tell.*
> *O come to us, abide with us,*
> *Our Lord, Emmanuel.*

HYMN FIVE:
O COME,
ALL YE FAITHFUL

John Francis Wade

O COME, ALL YE FAITHFUL

O come, all ye faithful, joyful and triumphant;
O come ye, O come ye to Bethlehem!
Come and behold Him—born the King of angels!

O come, let us adore Him!
O come, let us adore Him!
O come, let us adore Him—Christ, the Lord!

Sing, choirs of angels; sing in exultation;
O sing, all ye citzens of heaven above!
Glory to God, all glory in the highest!

O come, let us adore Him!
O come, let us adore Him!
O come, let us adore Him—Christ, the Lord!

Yea, Lord, we greet Thee, born this happy morning;
Jesus, to Thee be all glory given:
Word of the Father, now in flesh appearing!

O come, let us adore Him!
O come, let us adore Him!
O come, let us adore Him—Christ, the Lord!

CHAPTER 5

O COME, ALL YE FAITHFUL

"O come, all ye faithful, joyful and triumphant!"

The author of his hymn was John Francis Wade—at least his name is associated with the hymn. Scholars have debated whether the words are actually his or whether he used the words of someone else. Here is the story. In the 1700s, Wade roamed throughout Western Europe as a craftsman and as a proficient scribe who looked for odd jobs copying manuscripts. The requirements for the job were a good knowledge of spelling and a legible hand.

Wade got tired of copying the works of others and composed a Christmas carol in Latin that gained wide-spread prominence. He also claimed to compose the music for the hymn back in 1743. But some people insist that these words were sung in France before Wade was born and that the music sounds suspiciously like that of the great George Frederick Handel!

Yet other scholars insist that Wade is the author. Seven

manuscripts of the Latin stanzas were signed by Wade, and that might be proof enough that he did not plagiarize the words of someone else.

What is undisputed is that he inserted the song in the hymnal for the English Roman Catholic College in Bristol, Portugal. That act was the means by which the song was eventually spread around the world. Over the years, the Latin version underwent dozens of different translations into English, with some word changes that made it more favorable to Protestants. And in 1852, the hymn was given its present title, "O Come, All Ye Faithful."

This beautiful carol is an invitation to adore Christ. It is a song whose words are like arms outstretched, inviting the world to the stable in Bethlehem.

O come, let us adore Him!

Throughout history, not all have taken that opportunity. Others have come to adore Him at great personal cost. In Matthew 2, we have three different responses to the birth of Christ. Some adored Him, but others did not. Some even hated Him.

King Herod represents a jealous heart. He did not adore Christ for the simple reason that other things were more important to him. Herod was the great builder. Travel to Israel today and you will be impressed with the ruins of the Second Temple, built under his direction; there is also his palace and winter residence in Masada.

But King Herod was also cruel. He murdered two of his wives and one of his sons. We can surmise that he suffered from paranoia. He heard that a king had been born and he felt threatened—afraid of a baby! Even if the child would become king, that was years away. But that was of no comfort to Herod.

What set Herod off was the phrase, "king of the Jews." Herod was called "king" by the Roman Senate and he liked the title. To hear this description applied to someone else, even if a baby, ignited his jealousy. He was "troubled, and all Jerusalem with him" (Matthew 2:3). He coughed and all of Jerusalem caught a cold. No wonder the city was troubled, for no one knew what reaction Herod might have.

Why didn't he "come and adore Him?"

He was afraid that Christ might draw some attention away from him; after all, he was "king of the Jews." He loved the title, though it was not properly his. He was called "king" by the Roman Senate, but actually, he was only a half-Jew. Herod was an Idumaean, a descendant of Esau. Here we have the continuation of the old rivalry between Esau and Jacob that began when the twins were born.

First, Herod resorted to manipulation. He told the wise men that after they had found out about the King, they were to tell him so that he could "worship him also" (Matthew 2:8 KJV). That was a lie, of course. Jealous, controlling people always tell lies so that they can retain their position.

When he realized that they had tricked him by not returning, he was enraged and issued a decree that all the male children two years of age and younger were to be killed in the environs of Bethlehem. He would cast a wide net and be sure that this little baby would be included in his massacre. A powerful king intimidated by a baby!

As always, God had the last word. Herod died two years later. He had to give up the kingdom anyway; his jealousy did not permit him an extra day of rule. Even if Christ had taken away Herod's kingdom, it would not have mattered for very long.

Herod did not realize that his own power was derived from the baby in the manger; how much better if he had died adoring that baby.

One Christmas, I saw a toddler in a stroller with his hands on a little steering wheel. He turned it frantically to the left, but the stroller kept going to the right. His little steering wheel was not connected to anything that mattered. Turn it as he will, his mother controlled the direction he would go.

Sometimes we steer to the west and we go east; at other times we steer to the east and we go west. We have the illusion of control, but it is God who directs the affairs of men. Herod served as king according to the good pleasure of God—according to the will of the baby he hated. Herod said he wanted to adore Him but lied. Herod adored only himself.

The priests and the scribes had the opportunity to adore Him, but they were indifferent to the child in the manger. These were the men who preserved the law. They were the scholars, important gate-keepers in the synagogues because the common people were not educated. These were the leaders who told the common people what to believe.

How shall we characterize them?

Their status produced pride rather than humility. They knew the Scriptures so well that they numbered the letters and lines to make sure that they copied them carefully. Their knowledge of the law should have led them to treat God's law with open-mindedness and faith. But their knowledge was a barrier to understanding. The more they knew, the less they believed. They never bothered to check the remarkable story told by the wise men. The priests and the scribes mastered prophecy and geography, yet missed Him of whom the Scriptures spoke.

Later Jesus would say of them, "You search the Scriptures because you think that in them you have eternal life; and it is they that bear witness about me, yet you refuse to come to me that you may have life" (John 5:39, 40). The more they knew, the smaller they perceived their need to be. Their self-righteousness made them think they didn't need the Messiah, the Christ. They did not make the connection between their own need and the need for the Messiah. They would have welcomed someone to debate them, but didn't think they needed someone to cleanse them.

Kent Hughes writes, "they illustrate the amazing apathy to which religious people—those who have it all, have heard it all, and can recite it all—can fall into" (C.T. December 13, 1985, p. 28). Christmas can immunize us from Christ. The world hears just enough of the story each year to be inoculated; they catch the spirit of Christmas, but not the spirit of Christ. They see the words of Scripture, but misread their meaning.

Thankfully, the magi did adore Him. That word, "magi," is sometimes translated "wise men," and refers to a group of scholars who studied the stars. Their title connects them with magic, but they were probably astrologers. The magi came with real, but imperfect Messianic expectations.

We do not know if they were kings.

We do not know their number.

We do not know if they rode on camels.

We do not know how they heard about Christ.

We do not know how they identified the star.

Probably there were many of them in a large caravan. Only with such an impressive entry would Herod be troubled, "and all Jerusalem with him." Perhaps they heard about the Messiah because of the witness of Jews who had been spread abroad due to war and deportations.

God rewarded the willingness of these men to search out the truth. He gave them a special sign, a star that led them, but this is not an endorsement of astrology which is condemned elsewhere in the Scriptures. Speculation about the star has flourished for 2,000 years. Was it a supernova or was it a comet that moved in elliptical paths around the sun? Or possibly an alignment of planets? Such a positioning took place around 7 B.C. about two years before Christ's birth.

Whatever it was, this luminous wonder went and hovered over the location of the young child.

In fact, lest we become too enthusiastic about thinking that the Gospel might be in the stars, let us keep in mind that even the magi's experience was limited. We must emphasize that the star did not take them to Bethlehem. God did not bypass His Word. The star took them to Jerusalem, and there the priests and scribes looked up in the Old Testament where Christ was to be born.

Think of the barriers they had to overcome!

First, there was the barrier of distance. If they came from Persia as seems likely, they would have traveled about 1,000 miles and it might have taken them about a year to get to Bethlehem. When they arrive, Christ is not in a manger but in a house. And when Herod kills the male children, he chooses the age of two. That helps us understand the distance they traveled. Evidently they did not travel during the day;, they would have only traveled at night when the star shone.

They could have said, "It is too far to go!"

A second barrier they overcame was their race. Here are Persians bowing before a Jewish King, a baby at that! Despite the hostility between the two races, they accepted God's Jewish Messiah. Matthew wants us to understand that Jesus is not just the Messiah for the Jews, but also for the Gentiles. He is the King for the world. Whatever your race, you must accept the Jewish Messiah if you are to be saved.

They also overcame a religious barrier. They came from a country that had its own religion, astrology, occultism. They could have remained true to their heritage. I've heard people say, "I will die a Protestant, Catholic, or in the Jewish faith." Even if a particular church has left the truth, they will stay with it, no matter what!

Perhaps the most difficult barrier they overcame was their pride. They arrived rejoicing with noise and ecstasy. You can imagine them dismounting, straightening their robes and turbans, and stepping toward the entrance of the house. Martin Luther suggests that the humble dwelling was probably a great trial to them. Had they come thousands of miles to this, a poor peasant's home just outside the big city? To their everlasting credit, they entered.

Once inside, they didn't keep standing, nor did they

kneel. They "fell down" before the child, perhaps even lying prone before Him. Here are Gentiles bowing before a Jew. Even more—Gentiles bowing before a Jewish baby.

They worshipped Him. Literally that means, "to kiss toward." Here is intense adoration. Think of how the sight must have affected Joseph and Mary!

Then the gifts! Oh, the gifts, the treasures! They brought gold, frankincense, and myrrh. In ancient times, gifts were symbolical; you chose a gift that would suit the person. Consider what they brought: gold for a king, frankincense for a priest, myrrh for a sufferer.

If this interpretation is correct, they must have understood the full meaning of the Christ child. They returned to their home with the confidence that they had seen the One whom they hoped to see. These gifts would help Mary and Joseph as they soon would flee to Egypt to escape the Bethlehem massacre. Soon Mary and Joseph would grieve, knowing that it was because of their Son that other infants in the region were cruelly put to death. For now, that grief was far from their minds. They rejoiced that their Son was already honored as King.

I can imagine the magi leaving the house, hopping onto their camels and singing:

O come, let us adore Him!
O come, let us adore Him!
O come, let us adore Him—Christ, the Lord!

HYMN SIX:
AWAY IN A MANGER

Unknown

AWAY IN A MANGER

Away in a manger, no crib for a bed,
The little Lord Jesus laid down His sweet head.
The stars in the sky looked down where He lay;
The little Lord Jesus, asleep on the hay.

The cattle are lowing; the Baby awakes,
But little Lord Jesus—no crying He makes.
I love Thee, Lord Jesus; look down from the sky,
And stay by my side until morning is nigh.

Be near me, Lord Jesus; I ask Thee to stay
Close by me forever, and love me, I pray.
Bless all the dear children in Thy tender care,
And fit us for heaven, to live with Thee there.

ERWIN W. LUTZER

CHAPTER 6

AWAY IN A MANGER

No Christmas song is more loved than this tender children's carol. It is simple in expression and affirms the loving care of Mary and Joseph. It is a very touching scene that all of us have visualized: Mary wrapping her precious infant in strips of cloth and laying Him in a manger that had been used by the animals.

Away in a manger, no crib for a bed,
The little Lord Jesus laid down His sweet head.
The stars in the sky looked down where He lay;
The little Lord Jesus, asleep on the hay.

We do not know who wrote the first two stanzas of this carol. It first appeared in the Little Children's Book published in Philadelphia in 1885, but without the author's name listed. The third verse was written by John T. McFarland, a Methodist minister, because he needed an extra stanza for a Christmas program.

Many years ago, when I was on a secular radio program, I was asked whether I would believe that someone was the Son of God if He did the same miracles as Christ. My answer was: "it all depends on whether his whole life had the marks of the supernatural."

Christ's birth, life, death, and resurrection was a piece of whole cloth, stamped with the marks of divine intervention. We believe in Christ not just because of His miracles. His miracles are credible because there is so much other evidence that He was the Son of God.

Consider, for example, His birth. The shepherds were told by the angels, "This shall be a sign unto you." This was the first in a series of signs that Christ would give to those who desired to know God.

If the shepherds felt the sting of rejection, the fear of dying, and the emptiness of life itself, God provided someone who would be the Supreme Shepherd. He would do for His people what the shepherds did for their sheep. Yes, that night they would see a sign that they had met God's Messiah.

Since Bethlehem was a local center for tax collection and census, the Romans would have filled whatever few rooms that were available that night. They certainly would not have felt any compulsion to give up their beds for a Judean couple. Perhaps the second century tradition which says that Mary, Joseph, and the baby stayed in a cave which sheltered animals is correct. They spent the night where the sheep stayed in cold weather.

What was the sign that the shepherds were given?

First, that Christ was born in the right city. "For unto you is born this day in the city of David a Savior, who is Christ the Lord" (Luke 2:10, 11). The prophet Micah predicted that Bethlehem would be the town in which the Redeemer would be born. Christ came to "the house of bread" because He is the "bread of life."

Second, they would find the baby "wrapped in swaddling clothes," that is, strips of cloth. Mothers wrapped their newborns in these cloths which gave the infant a sense of security. The baby would know that he was loved and cared for.

What can we say about these cloths? They were ordinary rags, these were not fitting of a king; this is not purple and fine linen. He would never own His own wardrobe. And the borrowed clothes He did call His own would be gambled away. But for now, He lay helplessly in His mother's arms, feeding at her breast, and spending the night with the sheep. Mary is a peasant mother and she does what she has to do.

"You will find a baby wrapped in swaddling cloths and lying in a manger" (Luke 2:12). This was an unusual bed. Often a baby arrives to live in a room with his own furniture and toys. But there was none of this for Jesus. No designer shirts, no fancy shoes, no nursery with matching blue curtains. No musical toys and no sweet smells.

Christ was the only person born on this Earth who chose where He would be born. He and the Father worked out the details in ages long ago. What appeared to be a sad accident of history, was actually an act meticulously orchestrated by God. To be wrapped in swaddling clothes was not unusual, but to be in a manger was. The angel could have said, "I bring you good news, you'll find Him in room 777 in the Bethlehem Days Inn." But the sign was a manger.

This humble scene, "away in a manger," is so difficult to accept that we have reconstructed it to make it more suitable to our own tastes.

We have fumigated the stable.

The crib has been whitewashed.

The sheep are dry and clean.

The donkey is blow dried.

The carpet has been done by Stanley Steemer.

The baby has a halo around his head.

In fact, much as I like "Away in a Manger," there is one line with which I disagree. We sing, "The little Lord Jesus, no crying He makes." No, I believe He cried. He probably kept Mary and Joseph up late at night. He fussed and needed to be held.

Why the stable? Why the manger? Keep in mind it was

a sheep's crib. The Old Testament is filled with examples of God as our Shepherd. "Behold, I, I myself will search for my sheep and will seek them out...And I will set up over them one shepherd, my servant David, and he shall feed them" (see Ezekiel 34). Sheep are fed in a manger, thus Christ, the Chief Shepherd is born and lay where they would eat.

Keep in mind that it was also a borrowed crib. You could buy a crib, but nobody buys a manger. Mangers are built for animals and not purchased for babies. Mary and Joseph didn't own it, they just used it. Years later, Christ would say, "Foxes have holes, and birds of the air have nests, but the Son of Man has nowhere to lay his head" (Matthew 8:20). On the day He was born He didn't have a bed to call His own. Later, the tomb in which He was buried would also be borrowed.

Was Christ just living off the hard work of other people? Was He opposed to saving money and owning something? I don't think so. But He wanted to rebuke the materialism of the human heart. He wanted to demonstrate that our relationship with God is more important than the creature comforts which occupy so much of our time and energy. His humble birth was a final blow to the consumerism of every age, particularly our own.

Also, He wanted to affirm that whatever was given to Him was already His. As a human, He owned nothing, but as God, He owned it all. If He "owns the cattle on a thousand hills," He most assuredly owns the troughs from which they would eat. If He is the Creator of the mountains and rocks, He most assuredly would be the owner of the tomb in which He was placed.

Keep in mind that though He was in the manger, He had not lost His crown. The author of "Away in a Manger" was correct when he wrote, "I love Thee, Lord Jesus; look down from the sky." You would never sing that to an ordinary baby. But yes, this one could "look down from the sky, and stay by my side until morning is nigh."

The manger in the stable was improvised; it was pressed into service for something quite different than that for which it was built. Like a mother who takes curtains and sews them as dresses for her children, just so a manger was prepared to serve as a bed.

You mothers who are reading this—how would you react if you had to give birth in a stable and lay your newborn tenderly into a manger? How would you like to have your baby's first day spent in a room that smelled like a pet shop?

Why the manger? This was not accidental. "The manger was a sign telling us who Jesus was. It didn't just tell people where he was; the manger told who he was and what he had come to do" (Eternity, December 1979).

Why the manger?

A fatal blow to materialism, yes. But also a sign of the rejection which He would later have to endure. There was no room for them in the inn. Here is a woman in full term about to give birth and no one gives her a room!

Christ becomes attractive to those who have been rejected. We think of the drunkard who wandered into a barn one evening and awoke in the morning sleeping next to a cow. He heard the bells of Christmas and thought, "If Christ could be born and laid in a manger, maybe He can accept me." Maybe indeed.

Let us take one more look into the manger. I see poverty, I do not see riches. I see humiliation, not exaltation. I see the depths to which Christ was willing to come.

"My heart," someone has said, "is like that stable: dark, cold, and unclean; and though it was unworthy, it was chosen for the presence of the King."

"The first time he came, a star marked his arrival. The next time he comes, the whole heavens will roll up like a scroll, and all the stars will fall out of the sky, and he himself will light it.

"The first time he came, wise men and shepherds brought him gifts. The next time he comes, he will bring gifts, rewards for his own.

"The first time he came, there was no room for him. The next time he comes, the whole world will not be able to contain His glory.

"The first time he came, only a few attended his arrival—some shepherds and some wise men. The next time he comes, every eye shall see him.

"The first time he came as a baby. Soon he will come as Sovereign King and Lord." (*1500 Illustrations for Biblical Preaching,* Michael Green, editor).

He will go from the make-shift crib to the crown.

Until He returns, we sing:

Be near me, Lord Jesus; I ask Thee to stay
Close by me forever, and love me, I pray.
Bless all the dear children in Thy tender care,
And fit us for heaven, to live with Thee there.

Made in the USA
Columbia, SC
05 December 2021

50519366R00043